T0121012

SECTION 230

Free Speech and The Internet,
The Law that Makes it All Possible

PAUL M. STERNBERG
ATTORNEY-AT-LAW
WWW.THEDEFAMATIONATTORNEY.COM

authorHOUSE®

AuthorHouse™
1663 Liberty Drive
Bloomington, IN 47403
www.authorhouse.com
Phone: 833-262-8899

Published by AuthorHouse 01/12/2023

ISBN: 978-1-6655-7935-3 (sc)
ISBN: 978-1-6655-7936-0 (e)

Library of Congress Control Number: 2022924112

Print information available on the last page.

Any people depicted in stock imagery provided by Getty Images are models, and such images are being used for illustrative purposes only. Certain stock imagery © Getty Images.

This book is printed on acid-free paper.

DISCLAIMER

The information contained in this book are for general guidance on matters of interest only. The application and impact of laws can vary widely based on the specific facts involved. Given the changing nature of laws, rules and regulations, and the inherent hazards of updating printed material and electronic communication, there may be delays, omissions or inaccuracies in information contained in this book. Accordingly, the information in this book is provided with the understanding that the author and publisher are not herein engaged in rendering legal, accounting, tax, or other professional advice and services.

The author is NOT your attorney. As such, it should not be used as a substitute for consultation with professional accounting, tax, legal or other competent advisers. Before making any decision or taking any action, you should consult a professional. While the author has made every attempt to ensure that the information contained in this book have been obtained from reliable sources. The uthor is not responsible for any errors or omissions, or for the results obtained from the use of this information. All information in this book is provided, with no guarantee of completeness, accuracy, timeliness

ABOUT THE AUTHOR

Paul M. Sternberg, J.D. is in private practice at his own Houston, Texas law firm since 2001. He concentrates his practice in the areas of internet defamation law and business law. Mr. Sternberg is a graduate from the A.B.Freeman School of Business at Tulane University in 1987, and a 1996 graduate from South Texas College of Law in Houston, Texas where he was on the Dean's Honor Roll. Mr. Sternberg, a seasoned entrepreneur, is the author of THE GUIDE TO INTERNET DEFAMATION AND WEBSITE REMOVAL and THE GUIDE TO INVESTING IN COMMERCIAL REAL ESTATE. He has 10 years of experience on representing clients who have been the victims of defamatory cyber-attacks. Mr. Sternberg has developed a reliable blueprint in securing positive solutions in most cases. He has shared his professional knowledge with FOX NEWS and many other media outlets to discuss internet defamation. He is a frequent speaker to attorneys and community groups. He may be reached at www.TheDefamationAttorney. com or his office at 713-789-8120.

CONTENTS

INTRODUCTION
THE INTERNET AS WE KNOW IT TODAY

In the world we live in today, 85% of Americans are online daily. Of those, 31% report being online almost constantly, while 48% are "on" at least a few times a day. With social media, online shopping, mobile banking, and many other types of entertainment available at the touch of our fingertips, it's hard not to be "connected" 24/7. Even when we try to disconnect, those pesky notifications pull us right back in.

Although the internet has been around for a while, the invention of the Smartphone had a major impact on society. We now live in a digital world, where online presence is an integral part of both business and relationships.

Many people have even met their partners online through dating apps, or other connections. Big platforms like Twitter, Facebook, Instagram, and YouTube have become a central aspect of how people engage with clients and even make their livelihoods.

The freedom to express ourselves openly and creatively is what holds the threads of these enterprises together, and there is one thing that allows this current free-flowing system to thrive – Section 230.

The short and simple explanation is that Section 230 is the law that prevents large platforms from being held legally responsible for the content that users post on their sites. This keeps them from having to continuously monitor content to ensure no one is posting anything illegal or copyrighted and trademarked. Now, they moderate as much content as they can and try to stop anything that could be considered hate speech or fake news from circulating.

Platforms also take into consideration any reports about harassment, etc., and remove anything they find unacceptable. Sometimes accounts are suspended that are not following the rules -- without warning or explanation.

Section 230 came into question recently due to voices on the right feeling like they were being stifled on a lot of major platforms. It was thought that if the law were repealed Big Tech would no longer be able to limit what users were posting.

The actual result would be the opposite of that. If Section 230 were repealed those sites would have to monitor content even more than they do right now to prevent liability. However, this important law is now being examined and reevaluated by legislators on both sides and everyone needs to be aware of the potential outcomes any changes could bring about.

This guide will provide you with comprehensive information on all the ins and outs of this law, the history behind it, and the possible repercussions of repealing or amending any parts of it. It will also discuss how Section 230 relates to internet defamation lawsuits and provide some information on what steps citizens can take regarding the current legislative discussions.

* https://www.pewresearch.org/fact-tank/2021/03/26/about-three-in-ten-u-s-adults-say-they-are-almost-constantly-online/#:~:text=Overall%2C%2085%25%20of%20Americans%20say%20they%20go%20online,they%20do%20not%20use%20the%20internet%20at%20all.

CHAPTER 1
THE 1ST AMENDMENT AND FREEDOM OF SPEECH ON THE INTERNET

Whenever section 230 is discussed, it encourages reflection on the laws which first outlined freedom of speech in America. When the country was first beginning to form, leaders penned the Articles of Confederation. They were written with urgency during a time of war, and people were not yet comfortable with the idea of a new governing body. In those articles, states retained independence and sovereignty and Congress's purpose was treaty coordination, armed forces commandment, and dispute mediation. However, lawmakers realized those articles were missing a few necessary components, which lead to the convention of 1787, where the U.S. Constitution was drafted and signed.

The new document detailed basic rights for the people and became the supreme law of the land for the newly formed country. Dissolving the previous power of the states to act as their own countries, it established a stronger, unified government with three specific branches. The Executive, Judicial, and legislative branches were created to provide a system with checks and balances and prevent any person or group from having too much power.

After the Constitution was ratified, it became apparent that even more definition was needed regarding the freedoms of U.S. citizens. The Bill of Rights was created to declare the first 10 constitutional amendments.

Arguably, the first amendment to the Constitution is the most important. It reads, "Congress shall make no law respecting an establishment of religion or prohibiting the free exercise thereof: or abridging the freedom of speech, or the press; or the right of the people to assemble, and to petition the government for a redress of grievances."

That small fraction of a sentence gave us our right to have freedom of speech. It protects our ability to freely practice any religion we choose, publish intelligent and creative works, and come together to discuss important topics. It prevents government interference and prohibits any laws that impede any of these rights.

Our founding fathers knew how important these freedoms would be hundreds of years ago -- before computers or the idea of the internet ever existed. The freedom of expression was considered as essential as air to breathe – even then. As said in Paul Revere's iconic statement, "Give me liberty or give me death," right?

Free speech allows citizens to criticize people, places, and even the government – if they choose to. It protects people who voice their opinions regardless of the form of communication and helps uphold fair trade among companies and customers. If a business offers bad service or faulty products, their scam is usually revealed before it can affect a significant number of people, due to freedom of speech. Customers can go online and post reviews to save people from disappointment and wasted money. In this sense, it keeps people honest.

The freedom of expression also keeps the government in check. Political parties are under constant scrutiny and there are plenty of sources to report missteps by any branch of the government. In a Democracy, the government is ruled by the people, and without freedom of speech that wouldn't be possible.

However, the right to speak our minds and voice our opinions isn't meant to protect liars and defamers. If an internet platform like Instagram wants to ban someone for posting things that violate their terms of agreement, they have the power to do so, as does any other website. However, they don't usually get involved in possible defamation cases. An example of this would be making a false claim against a company or an individual for personal gain. Although it is an offense that can impede businesses and damage their reputation, platforms won't allow themselves to be caught in the middle. Defamatory attacks limit the credibility of products and service providers -- causing a domino effect of negative outcomes for any business. A person or business that feels they have been defamed would most likely have to pursue legal help to have any content removed from a social media site.

Free speech is a powerful privilege that isn't recognized globally. In many areas of the world, the public has no way to speak out against a harmful government without fear of punishment. We are fortunate to live in a country that affords us these rights. However, our government draws a line when the free speech of one individual is harmful to another because it isn't truthful.

The freedom to express our thoughts and opinions without fear of retribution is one of the things that led to the popularity of all the social media sites we enjoy today. Most people positively use these platforms, sharing things with their family and friends or promoting their products or businesses. But some people troll these sites looking to wreak havoc on others and create unnecessary conflict. This has been witnessed a lot more over the past few years, especially during the global Pandemic. This period of isolation, political controversy, and economic instability has people on edge and slinging mud back and forth more than ever.

The current atmosphere can be a breeding ground for hostility, which increases the potential for more harmful content. Platforms do try to regulate what is posted on their sites, but it is very time-consuming and nearly impossible for them to monitor everything. There are ways for users to report offensive posts and have them taken down or the accounts suspended, but there is plenty of harmful content that still goes unregulated.

SECTION 230

This brings us to the state of limbo we are now in with the laws surrounding freedom of expression and the internet.

The debate surrounding section 230 remains. Voices on both sides feel that changes should be made but coming to an agreement regarding those changes continues to be a challenge. Anything that is changed could irrevocably alter our current society and have an impact on the rest of the world. This is not a decision that should be taken lightly or rushed through litigation. Those on both sides must examine every detail and imagine all potential outcomes before taking any action. Legislators must analyze the history, and specific cases relating to defamation, and try to envision the future consequences should any of the language of Section 230 be removed or altered in any way.

CHAPTER 2
WHAT IS SECTION 230 OF THE COMMUNICATIONS DECENCY ACT?

A lot of people have heard of section 230 as it's been a big topic of discussion over the last few years. However, not everyone knows what it is. Ultimately, it's the 26-word law in the Common Decency Act of 1996 that allows the internet to function as it does today. It reads that "No provider or user of an interactive computer service shall be treated as the publisher or speaker of any information provided by another information content provider."

Breaking that down means that platforms like Twitter, Facebook, Instagram, and YouTube cannot be held legally responsible for the content that users post on their sites. Therefore, they are not liable for any defamatory comments and cannot be sued by individuals or businesses that are hurt by libelous content. For example, if a customer posts a negative review about a business on Yelp, that business cannot file a lawsuit against Yelp for defamation. Yelp is not considered the publisher of the content that the customer posted on their website.

Websites do monitor content to the best of their abilities and try to remove anything harmful or suspend accounts that go against their terms of service, but they are not able to moderate all content. Twitter alone has billions of users and most of them tweet multiple times a day. It would be almost impossible to regulate such a high volume of content.

At the time Section 230 was created, the world had no idea what the internet would look like today. However, two significant cases showed the legal system in place at the time was not equipped to handle liability issues stemming from online sources. Cubby vs. Compuserve (1991) and Straton Oakmont vs. Prodigy (1995) spurred the creation of the CDA in the 1990s.

In the first case, the defendant, CompuServe, was an online service that hosted forums. One of the publications available to subscribers was a daily newsletter called *Rumorville,* by Dan Fitzpatrick. The plaintiff, Robert Blanchard, owner of Cubby, Inc., sued Fitzpatrick for posting defamatory remarks about his newsletter, *Skuttlebut.* He also sued CompuServe for hosting the content.

Cubby argued that CompuServe had acted as *Rumorville*'s publisher and was therefore liable for Fitzpatrick's statements. But since CompuServe didn't have any prior knowledge of the contents of *Rumorville*, did not control its publication, and didn't review the newsletter's contents, the U.S. District Court ruled that CompuServe had acted as a distributor, not a publisher, and was therefore not liable.

The distinction between publishers, which are liable for the statements they circulate, and distributors—such as a bookstore or a newsstand—which are not, emerged from the Supreme Court case *Smith v. California* (1959). In that case, a bookseller named Eleazer Smith was convicted of violating a Los Angeles city ordinance criminalizing the possession of obscene books. He appealed it and the Supreme Court agreed that it was unconstitutional. If ordinances like that were permitted every bookseller would need to make themselves aware of the contents of every book in their shop and expecting someone to be omniscient is unreasonable.

Jordan Belfort founded Stratton Oakmont in 1986 as a brokerage firm specializing in trading "over-the-counter" securities. The film *The Wolf of Wall Street* was based on this story. Prodigy Services was an early online service network that provided its subscribers access to various information services such as bulletin boards where third parties exchanged information. Prodigy, unlike CompuServe, had "held itself out" as exercising editorial control over the content of its computer bulletin boards. One of Prodigy's bulletin boards was called *Money Talk*, a popular forum where members would post and discuss financial matters.

On October 23rd and 25th in 1994, an unidentified individual posted to the *Money Talk* bulletin board claiming that Stratton Oakmont committed criminal and fraudulent acts in connection with an IPO that it was involved in. Stratton Oakmont and Daniel Porush filed suit against Prodigy in the New York Supreme Court, the state trial court, alleging libel, among other things.

The court concluded that Prodigy was indeed a "publisher." Reasoning that Prodigy "held itself out" to the public and its members as controlling the content of *Money Talk*.

Although they had originally intended to moderate their content, the network became too popular, and they could not keep up. Section 230 was born because of the conflict between these two cases. It didn't seem fair that the service provider that tried to moderate content was found liable and the one that didn't moderate any content was not. Therefore, the Common Decency Act was formed to provide a framework for similar cases going forward and encourage sites to at least attempt to moderate some content.

These cases all had an impact on the way everything works today and affords platforms the protections they currently enjoy. Websites not having to be responsible to moderate all content on their sites allows users the freedom of expression we all enjoy. Social media has allowed businesses a way to thrive like never before and paved the way for many new career paths. There are a lot of people who make their living as influencers, social media managers, and online marketers. Businesses use multiple platforms to build relationships with potential customers daily.

This is all due to one law created 25 years ago. However, legislators seek to reform or change it, but can't seem to agree on the specifics. Some think that it allows sites the ability to regulate too much content that isn't aligned with their viewpoint. That was former President Trump's issue with Section 230. He felt that voices on the Right were being silenced by platforms that identified more with the Left politically. The question was raised as to the amount of censorship being allowed on the internet. Were these actions limiting the public's right to freedom of speech, or were these sites simply trying to eliminate content that violated their terms of service?

Others felt that there wasn't enough moderation going on and the unregulated content incited hatred and violence, leading to things like the insurrection. As the political climate shifts, the question of whether section 230 is operating as it was intended remains. Many believe that the language isn't clear enough and that a more concise definition needs to be outlined.

As we learned from the two original cases that led to this law's creation, legislators wanted platforms to moderate content to the best of their ability but didn't want them to be punished for missing something. No matter what changes are made, the way we currently operate as a society could have global consequences as other countries often follow in our footsteps. Section 230 doesn't just affect the big platforms like Twitter, Facebook, Instagram, YouTube, TikTok, and Amazon. It regulates every dating site, job board, forum, and application we use today.

If lawmakers do decide that further clarification is needed, they must be very careful with the verbiage and mindful of the repercussions it may cause. If it is decided that online platforms need to be held more accountable for the content that users post on their sites, they will be forced to moderate more. That will cost them a lot of time and money and could result in a loss of freedom of speech on the internet. On the slip side of that, if the language is changed to take the ability to regulate away, there could be a lot more defamation, hate speech, and fake news circulating. Section 230 has worked quite well over the last quarter of a century, but there are a few cases that might be used to call for change.

* https://www.eff.org/issues/cda230

* https://thedefamationattorney.com/is-section-230-operating-as-intended/

* https://mtsu.edu/first-amendment/article/415/smith-v-california

* https://wjlta.com/2022/02/18/stratton-oakmont-v-prodigy-services-the-case-that-spawned-section-230/

CHAPTER 3
HOW DOES THIS LAW AFFECT INTERNET DEFAMATION CASES?

After learning the basics of section 230, one might wonder how it affects internet defamation cases. The law impacts different cases in several ways.

First, it depends on whether a case is civil or criminal. Many online defamation cases are considered a tort, or civil suit. Most internet defamation cases are solely brought against the individual or business that posted the content because of how section 230 immunities work for big tech companies. However, there are times when a victim will ask the platform to take down the harmful content and the social media company does not act upon the request. It is either ignored entirely or a response stating that the post doesn't break their rules of conduct is sent. In these instances, a party may bring forth a claim with the platform as an interested party, but they cannot file a claim against the platform.

Other civil claims against platforms stem from advertising, providing adult content to minors, nuisance, negligence, and discrimination. Social media platforms are protected by section 230 in these cases as it maintains that the sites may not have known about the content posted. Although if paid ads are being placed on a site, one would hope they are being monitored.

These immunities only apply in civil cases. When it comes to criminal cases, section 230 does not protect social media companies. Some examples of criminal claims might be cases involving copyright infringements, sexual exploitation of children, or other sex crimes.

Social Media companies are under heavy scrutiny for mishandling hate speech and allowing the spread of fake news. Since society is starting to get much of their news from social media, big tech companies might need to take more responsibility for what is posted on their sites. Most platforms rely on a mixture of both automated and human intervention to regulate content. However, the sheer volume shared on social media makes it nearly impossible to establish a comprehensive system. Using Twitter as an example, it is estimated that there are approximately 500 million tweets sent per day. If an average tweet is 20 words long, the volume of the content on Twitter in one day is equal to 182 years of what is published by the New York Times. The capability of monitoring that much content is beyond the scope of current technology, but there are still some ways platforms could do better.

Facebook relies on users to flag content and then uses a human team to monitor and determine if posts violate its terms of use. Live content is also monitored once it reaches a certain level of popularity. Artificial intelligence helps monitor textual content in real-time, and sensitive content is being detected by algorithms, but human eyes are still needed in certain situations.

Since Section 230 provides a certain level of immunity, the consensus is that these companies are not as concerned about what's being posted as they should be. It is believed that they would regulate better if held accountable for the content posted on their sites.

In 2020, the EARN IT act was proposed but did not pass. However, it's back with a vengeance. The Eliminating Abusive and Rampant Neglect of Interactive Technologies Act passed unanimously in the Senate Judiciary Committee and has wide bipartisan support in Congress. The legislation will encourage the tech industry to take online child sexual exploitation seriously and removes blanket immunity of laws related to online child sexual abuse material (CSAM).

The bill amends section 230 of the CDA to remove immunity for service providers when it comes to combating child sexual exploitation and eradicating CSAM, creating accountability. It's based on the belief that tech companies should be held responsible for their complicity in the sexual abuse and exploitation of children when they refuse to report or remove images of these crimes hosted on their platforms.

The EARN IT Act has the backing of more than 250 groups including the National Center for Missing & Exploited Children (NCMEC), Rights4Girls, the National

Center on Sexual Exploitation, National District Attorneys Association, National Association of Police Organizations, Rape, Abuse & Incest National Network, International Justice Mission, and Major Cities Chiefs Association.

The legislation also seeks to establish a National Commission of Online Child Sexual Exploitation Prevention that will be responsible for developing best practices. The Commission includes the heads of the DOJ, DHS, FTC, and 16 other members appointed by congressional leadership, including reps from law enforcement, survivors and victim's services organizations, constitutional law experts, tech, and industry experts.

The bill bolsters recourse for survivors and tools for enforcement. However, the law also places a lot of power to regulate internet providers directly in the hands of state legislatures. It would outsource the key decision-making power to a politically chosen body. The committee would involve the Attorney General, Secretary of Homeland Security, and appointees with a background in law enforcement. There is concern that the group is not a representative of the broader issue and would not be accountable for the decisions it makes.

The lack of accountability coupled with the fact that the bill repeats many of the mistakes found in the FOSTA/SESTA laws has advocacy groups concerned that the law's broad scope could be used to erode basic online freedoms at the whims of politicians. The bill states that the use of encryption could be a reason to lose liability protection and the power handed to the committee means a change in leadership could easily remove encryption for good.

It was for this reason that the bill was strongly condemned by the American Civil Liberties Union and many advocates for online civil liberties, sex workers, and LGBT rights activists. It is argued that it would encourage companies to abandon strong encryption and privacy protections for users.

The Electronic Frontier Foundation, along with 60 other human rights, civil rights, and open internet organizations sent a letter to the Senate Judiciary Committee outlining their concerns with the EARN IT Act because it threatens encryption and free speech while making it more difficult to protect children from online abuse.

No matter how great a bill may sound, there is always more to it than what meets the eye, which is why there will be groups on both sides of every issue.

* https://www.brookings.edu/research/the-politics-of-section-230-reform-learning-from-fostas-mistakes/

*https://www.brookings.edu/blog/techtank/2021/03/17/back-to-the-future-for-section-230-reform/?msclkid=95fc3543b9a211ecae5501c387b52f66

*https://www.engadget.com/earn-it-act-2022-explained-153058123.html?guccounter=1

*https://www.omnicoreagency.com/twitter-statistics/

CHAPTER 4
EXAMPLES

Let's look at a few examples of how section 230 has impacted real cases.

FACEBOOK VS. WINTER

In July 2021, Plaintiffs Elliot Winter and Alexandria Hurlburt filed an action against Defendants Facebook, Inc. ("Facebook"); TikTok Inc., TikTok PTE Ltd., Bytedance Ltd., and Bytedance Inc. ("TikTok"); and Monica Dolan ("Dolan"), in the Circuit Court of St. Louis, Missouri. Plaintiffs alleged that Dolan and others associated with her engaged in a pattern of behavior that resulted in the harassment of the Plaintiffs on her social media accounts and because of Facebook and TikTok's failure to take down false abusive posts and/or posts containing the plaintiff's personal identifying information used for stalking and harassment. Plaintiffs sustained damages that exceed $500.000.00 and asserted claims against Dolan for defamation – slander; defamation – libel; tortious interference with business contract and expectancy; invasion of privacy; false light; intentional infliction of emotional distress;

stalking; harassment; and unlawful posting of certain information over the internet; and a single claim of "gross negligence" against Facebook and Tiktok.

Both Facebook and TikTok moved to dismiss the motions against them. The purpose of rule 12(b)(6) is to dismiss an action for failure to state a claim and test the legal sufficiency of a complaint to eliminate actions that are flawed and sure to fail – sparing the burden of unnecessary litigation. The plaintiff does not need to provide specific facts in support of the allegations but must include sufficient information to provide the "grounds" on which the claim rests. This standard calls for enough facts to raise a reasonable expectation that discovery will reveal evidence of the claim. Facebook and TikTok argued that the plaintiffs' negligence claim against them should be dismissed because the claim is barred by section 230, and the plaintiffs have failed to show facts establishing the existence of a duty that Facebook or TikTok owed them.

To determine whether Section 230 immunity applies, a court must ensure the defendant is a provider of an interactive computer service; the information for which the plaintiff seeks to hold the defendant liable is provided by another information content provider, or the plaintiff's claim treats the defendant as a publisher of the information. In this case, all three elements were satisfied.

The Court found that the Plaintiffs' claim regarding the platform's refusal to remove the content and accounts posted by Dolan and her group is barred under Section 230 of the CDA. The cases against Facebook and TikTok were dismissed.

Section 230 protected the platforms in this case and functioned as it was intended, but there are cases where Section 230 immunity does get called into question.

HERRICK VS. GRINDR

Consider the 2017 case brought by Matthew Herrick against Grindr. In 2016, Hundreds of strangers began showing up at Matthew Herrick's home and work in New York City, looking for sex. The strangers were not invited by Herrick, they were directed to him by fake profiles on the geosocial network Grindr. The lawsuit alleged that the profiles, which in some cases instructed suitors to understand resistance by Herrick was part of an agreed-upon rape fantasy, were created by his vengeful ex-boyfriend — and that despite more than 100 complaints, a cease-and-desist letter, and a court injunction, Grindr failed to stop the ex-boyfriend from abusing its application.

Grindr filed a motion to dismiss the lawsuit, citing Section 230 immunity under the CDA. Section 230 has done a great job of shielding big tech companies from a wide array of liability claims, but for victims of online harassment or abuse, it has meant tech companies bear no legal responsibility to help them when company platforms are being used to facilitate their torment.

Herrick's lawyers argued that Grindr did not qualify for section 230 immunity because the claim that it was technologically unable to block the offender from abusing its application – despite the availability of such technology -- was evidence of negligence and created an unreasonable danger to the public.

Grindr is an LGBTQ dating app that is used daily by millions of people worldwide, and it could have tried harder to protect Herrick. Competing applications can block similar types of abusers within 24 hours of notification. The Plaintiffs argued that Grindr was somewhat liable for the abuse due to its failure to stop it.

A judge determined that Section 230 granted Grindr immunity and dismissed the lawsuit. But it's important to recognize that Grindr could have prevented the ongoing abuse and should have anticipated the app's risks and developed the technology to mitigate abuse of its product. Grindr could have used technologies like user verification, VPN blocking, and photo DNA analysis to protect its users, but they didn't bother because they knew they could use CDA as a shield.

With the ability to hide behind Section 230, the tech industry doesn't ever have to worry about seeing the inside of a courtroom and faces no liability to the public for the weaponization of their products -- and that is a cause for concern.

Other cases are pending right now of large accounts being banned from Twitter without warning or violating any of Twitter's policies. There is concern that unfair censorship is happening while at the same time, users have reported accounts for threats and other abusive content, and nothing is done. It is suggested that platforms are picking and choosing the content they wish to moderate without consideration of the impact on its users, and any cases against them are thrown out due to Section 230 before an in-depth look at discovery occurs.

As social media continues to grow, the laws should change and adapt along with it. If a tech company has a way to protect its users from abuse, there should be repercussions if they refuse to do so. The question remains as to how to go about the legality. Do lawmakers restructure Section 230, or do they create new legislation to deal with specific instances that come up?

The legal system is slow at making changes because what may seem like a small thing can create a much larger web of ramifications than anyone intended.

* https://casetext.com/case/winter-v-facebook-inc/

* https://www.buzzfeednews.com/article/tylerkingkade/grindr-herrick-lawsuit-230-online-stalking

CHAPTER 5
WHY DO LAWMAKERS WANT TO REPEAL OR CHANGE IT?

Section 230 came under the gun from President Trump before the election in 2020. He accused tech firms of using the law as a shield to disguise political partisan activity. Republican lawmakers alleged that conservative voices were silenced by platforms banning users for "breaking" site rules. They claim section 230 has little to do with censorship and simply allows private internet companies to be selective about the content and users they want on their platforms.

Current President, Joe Biden, also wants major changes made to section 230. He believes the law has not done enough to shield people from false information on the internet. He feels platforms are propagating known falsehoods. Fellow democrats argue that big social media companies have failed to regulate hate speech and fake news on their sites.

Both sides want to reform section 230 for different reasons. The right believes there is too much moderation, and the left thinks there isn't enough. The debate continues as lawmakers try to agree.

Prominent voices all along the political spectrum blame the law for a variety of real and perceived harms on the Internet; including harassment, hate speech, disinformation, violent content, child sexual abuse material, and nonconsensual pornography.

There have been a few recent amendments to section 230. In 2018, the Fight Online Sex Trafficking Act and Stop Enabling Sex Traffickers Act were passed. FOSTA/ SESTA states that if websites knowingly assist, support, facilitate, or actively violate federal sex trafficking laws they can be held legally liable. There was a lot of support on both sides for the bill; however, studies suggest that it placed sex workers at an increased risk. Without websites for advertising and communication, those in the sex trade were forced back out on the streets. Additionally, the law may have hindered the ability to investigate and prosecute trafficking.

Lawmakers don't seem inclined to review FOSTA/SESTA when discussing additional section 230 reform, but they should. It's important to look at the way websites respond to the new legislature and the impact on society. The recent amendments are a great case study to project how changes will affect the internet as we know it.

The current options regarding section 230 are to preserve it, repeal it, or reform it. The best approach may be for Congress to pass targeted reforms addressing specific parts without causing too much disruption to the way the Internet functions. However, the voices that want to repeal or dismantle it scream the loudest. Thankfully, our system of checks and balances makes it more challenging to change anything quickly and requires a lot of support from both the left and the right before any decisions are made.

However, if policymakers are unable to agree, the Supreme Court may act in Congress's place. In 1997 a notice and takedown policy was rejected, but it may be worth reconsidering now. The idea proposed that Section 230 immunity would not apply if a service provider received adequate notice about illegal material and failed to act. The court thought it was inconsistent with Section 230's purpose to encourage platforms to self-regulate content. The judges thought notice liability would lead to excessive content removal. A notice and takedown system might be more effective in policing illegal content than immunizing companies for their failure to act, which is what the current statute allows.

Another bipartisan approach to Section 230 reform involves piecemeal carve-outs that focus on online harms and illegality. An example of this would include withdrawing immunity for content connected to civil rights violations or international terrorism.

Democratic senators Amy Klobuchar, Mazie Hirono, and Mark R. Warner introduced the Safeguarding Against Fraud; Exploitation, Threats, Extremism, and Consumer Harms Act, also known as Safe Tech. The Safe Tech act would ensure section 230 protections wouldn't apply to ads or other paid content, doesn't interfere with the enforcement of civil rights laws, or impair laws addressing stalking, cyber-stalking, harassment, or intimidation, and doesn't bar wrongful death suits or bar suits under the Alien Tort Claims act. Perhaps the most crucial element of the Safe Tech act, and all other Section 230 reform proposals is that they do not guarantee that platforms will be held liable, but they ensure that victims have an opportunity to raise claims without Section 230 immunity impeding their ability to seek justice.

Proposals that pick and choose among the possible sources of litigation against social media companies with a carve-out approach increase the burden of legal analysis to determine if platforms have immunity in particular cases. It creates an open-ended drive for Congress to update Section 230 exceptions every time egregious harm is immunized by a broad interpretation of the law. Piecemeal proposals decrease the likelihood of gaining bipartisan agreement on any given measure.

Some proposals are focused on modifying Section 230's requirement that platforms act in "good faith" when they remove content. However, that idea misunderstands how Section 230 works. Section 230 doesn't help platforms win cases after lengthy court proceedings; it allows those cases to be dismissed before wasting time and money on unnecessary litigation.

One suggestion is to condition Section 230 immunity on a regulatory finding of a platform's political neutrality, but others want to make the immunity contingent on a court's determination of reasonable content moderation practices. However, these requirements do not need to be tied to Section 230. These policy ideas could be mandated directly as new legislation for social media companies.

Section 230 may not be the right vehicle for addressing issues that could be resolved by crafting a regulatory framework for platforms. Reforming the statute will not resolve how social media controls legal but harmful information, including hate speech or fake news, which are protected by the first amendment. It might be the wrong mechanism to impose transparency and accountability for content moderation or violations of a platform's rules involving legal speech.

The basis of Section 230 reform is about the extent to which platforms should be liable for illegal speech and activity users post on their sites – not about any other regulatory issues. Both sides agree that there is too much illegal and harmful material on social media which could be eliminated by reforming the current system.

https://itif.org/publications/2021/02/22/proposals-reform-section-230/

https://www.brookings.edu/blog/techtank/2021/03/17/back-to-the-future-for-section-230-reform/

https://royalexaminer.com/warner-announces-the-safe-tech-act-to-reform-section-230/

CHAPTER 6
IF CHANGED OR REPEALED, WHAT MIGHT HAPPEN?

"If you have ever forwarded an email -- whether a news article, a party invitation, or birth announcement -- you have done so with the protection of Section 230." – Dr. Corynne McSherry, Legal Director of the Electronic Frontier Foundation.

Those outspoken about repealing Section 230 often only look at the positives and never consider the fallout from such a monumental change.

Some want to repeal Section 230 because they want less censorship on social media, and others want more power to reign in Big Tech. Unfortunately, the reality would likely disappoint both sides.

Yes, it would hold platforms more accountable to stop the spread of fake news, hate speech, and other harmful content. And it would decrease the amount of defamation and harassment that takes place online -- but there are a lot of factors to consider. Section 230 doesn't just protect Big Tech companies; it protects everyone and allows the free speech we've come to take for granted.

Without Section 230 immunity, sites that host user-generated content would have two options to avoid liability. They would either need to moderate zero content and only remove things as required by law or moderate aggressively, censoring anything that could pose a liability risk.

Large platforms like Twitter, Google, and Facebook have already demonstrated the desire to censor beyond the legal requirements and would likely choose to clamp down on censorship and remove everything they could potentially be liable for. They know their users want moderation and allowing a free-for-all approach would provide a bad user experience and drive advertisers away. Smaller platforms would crumble as they don't have the means to combat lawsuits or pay additional staff to maintain the level of moderation they would need to survive.

If Section 230 is killed without proper thought to what comes next, then big chunks of the internet will become unusable. Platforms would have to use extreme caution by censoring anything that could prompt a legal issue or shutting down comments completely.

Repealing section 230 would provoke a flurry of cases for every major site and case law would determine the fate of the internet in the absence of statute; however, there aren't many cases to look to as a standard since Section 230 has been such a large obstacle for any potential lawsuits in the past.

Smaller sites, which can't absorb litigation costs and lack the money to implement comprehensive moderation, will be in serious jeopardy. Any repeal would likely force sites to take a heavy-handed approach, removing more speech than necessary.

We've already caught glimpses of this with FOSTA/SESTA, which forced platforms to mass-censor adult content. Because of the legal risk of hosting the material, many sites issued blanket bans, like Tumblr, which saw its user numbers plummet in the process. YouTube demonetized and suppressed educational material for LGBTQ teens.

AI carries biases, lacks nuance, and is very bad at determining context. For example, Facebook banned nipples, which excluded all breastfeeding pictures too.

Any website that relies on user-generated content would be in trouble. For example, with Section 230, Yelp can do whatever it wants with negative reviews. But without it, Yelp has two choices: fight the onslaught of legal cases from bad reviews or take the content down. If Yelp starts to remove all its negative reviews to stay out of legal trouble, then it loses its value. It would become redundant, and no one would use it anymore.

Sites like Amazon thrive on Section 230, allowing reviews they are not held liable for. They would need to moderate every single review or get rid of them completely to avoid the risk. If Section 230 were repealed, we would be saying goodbye to reviews *everywhere*.

Social Media sites would probably need to pre-approve every single post and/or comment. Facebook, Twitter, and a few other large networks are the only ones with the money and staff to be able to moderate that much content. A new social network wouldn't be able to compete without a huge budget built-in for that.

Those upset over occasionally getting "fact-checked" on Twitter, would now need to have every tweet be pre-approved, losing that instant communication channel to the world.

Sites like Wikipedia, which are all about user-generated content, would cease to exist. Anywhere you can post on someone else's site, your ability to do that would be reduced or removed. That means no more wishing your friends a Happy Anniversary on their date night pictures either.

Given the current political climate and the partisan nature of both politics and law in the US, we can't assume that judges would be ready to defend the status quo. It's likely that, while the system has numerous flaws and allows bad actors to flourish, the alternative could be much worse.

Are we willing to give up all our reviews and commentary to alter the scope with which we see the digital world? Do we want to give up the free speech we enjoy today? Is protecting ourselves from fake news, hate speech, and online harassment worth never seeing a difference of opinion or being able to engage in intelligent discourse?

Those that wish to reign in Big Tech will be sadly mistaken, as revoking section 230 will surely crush all the small fish in the pond, making the large platforms even more powerful as our only resources of online information.

Sadly, most people have never heard of Section 230, and if they have, they are either completely misinformed or have never thought about the bigger picture. We can't simply remove a law that has allowed the internet to function the way it has for the last 26 years without major ramifications. As discussed in previous chapters, adding specific legislation for certain circumstances is probably the most effective way to make the changes society needs with the least amount of damage. Therefore, every aspect needs to be considered and discussed by lawmakers before taking any action. If the entire law were dismantled, the world would no longer function the way we know it today.

https://www.engadget.com/2020-01-31-s230-repeal.html

CHAPTER 7
WHAT HAS HAPPENED ELSEWHERE IN THE WORLD?

When we discuss repealing section 230, we need to look at other countries that actively censor the internet. The U.S. is free compared to Russia, China, or India with new regulations cracking down on "mischievous information", and even Germany – which has a rigorous ban on hate speech.

Russia has made steps toward cutting itself off from the global internet. President Vladimir Putin signed a law that requires all computers, smartphones, and smart TVs sold in Russia to come pre-loaded with apps from Russian developers. The government also invested the equivalent of $32 million into a Russian Wikipedia alternative. These changes along with the isolationist infrastructure suggest the desire for more control over the Russian people and a disconnection from the rest of the world. It was already seen that the people of Russia were not up to date with the war in Ukraine in 2022. The people are largely misinformed about the War and that's a cause for concern. Although Russia is not completely cut off from the rest of the world, the current partial censorship and laws produce a chilling effect.

The Russian government has built legal and infrastructure internet-level controls to establish content filters and block lists and introduce oversight mechanisms within private telecoms. During the political protests of 2018, the Russian government cut mobile data services. There was another internet blackout in August of 2021 in Moscow. Technical issues have prevented full isolation, but it appears that's the goal of the Russian President.

In China, their firewall gives the government almost total control over the internet, but censorship was there from the beginning. It's much harder to go backward and install mechanisms for control in a country where the internet grew unchecked for decades. Russia has tried and failed to ban encrypted messaging apps and crack down on VPNs.

The Chinese-controlled internet is completely different from that used by the rest of the globe. The censorship blocks users in China from many of the apps and websites used in the U.S. or other countries. A virtual private network is needed to access Google, Facebook, Instagram, or Twitter. A Chinese phone cannot download Western apps. The VPN would need to be installed outside of China, before entering the country.

There are also strict ID regulations, and some apps require a selfie holding a passport next to your face along with the picture of the passport to be sent to the app.

It's like passing through customs to use their internet. Everything you do is saved on your device, linked to your face, location, bank account, and ID. It's one more way for the government to track people, in addition to cameras and facial recognition software.

In China, most of the news is state media. The same headlines appear in every paper. If you read or watch the news, there are about 20 minutes of good news about China, and 10 minutes of bad news about the rest of the world. It's joked about but it does affect the worldview of the people. Many Chinese citizens believe that China is safe, but the U.S. is dangerous. The people know they are censored. It's common for a post to disappear within 10 minutes because of the content, or to not be able to post something at all. There is a cultural bias happening due to the level of control over information.

Germany's Network Enforcement Law, NetzGD, requires social media companies to remove content that violates one of twenty restrictions on hate and defamatory speech in the German Criminal Code with millions of euros in fines at stake.

It's not surprising that countries like Turkey and Venezuela would emulate the intrusive legislation. French legislators attempted to do the same, and lawmakers in the U.K. are debating the very broad powers associated with a similar legislative model that introduces the concept of "legal but harmful online speech" which is speech that we may disagree with but is currently legal in a free society.

Austria is also considering a NetzDG-inspired law that would further encourage compliance by forbidding businesses who advertise on those platforms to pay what's owed if they aren't operating under the law.

Lawmakers in Brazil are considering a campaign against "fake news" which is vague on the definition and is described as false or deceptive content shared with the potential to cause an individual or collective harm. It's concerning how much power that could give those in the government to manipulate the term for political gain.

In Pakistan, there was a law passed in 2016 that granted the government the power to censor online content and criminalize hate speech and defamation. It was part of a plan to combat terrorism in response to an attack on a school that killed more than 130 children.

The implementation was supposed to help defend the country against threats to national security and cybercrime, but the broadly defined provisions meant that it could be used to limit online expression and voices that were critical of the government. Since the passing of PECA (Prevention of Electronic Crimes Act), it has been used against journalists and women who have come forward with allegations of sexual harassment online. There have been charges of defamation brought against them. A U.S. State Department's human rights report from 2021 concluded that it gave the government in Pakistan sweeping powers to censor content on the internet which has been used by authorities to clamp down on civil society.

The Pakistan government has repeatedly tightened control and has banned dating apps over supposed "immoral content" and imposed penalties including fines and bans on social media platforms that violate government requests to take down content.

Most of the debate in the US has focused on the domestic impact of a post Section 230 internet but eliminating the law could have global consequences. It could set a precedent for even more countries to make new policies and place restrictions on digital speech or make platforms liable for content posted on their sites, causing aggressive moderation. If the U.S. stops fighting for free speech online, then the rest of the world might follow.

Whether we like it or not we are often the role model of "freedom". It's what our whole country was founded upon and the further we move away from that concept, the more we give permission for other countries to do the same. If the "Land of the Free" isn't free, why should anyone else be?

*https://www.wired.com/story/russia-internet-control-disconnect-censorship/

*https://www.latimes.com/world/la-fg-us-china-internet-split-20190603-story.html

*https://reason.com/2020/10/12/german-style-internet-censorship-catches-on-around-the-world/

*https://www.rappler.com/technology/features/global-consequences-united-states-section-230-coda-story/

CHAPTER 8
WHAT WOULD THESE CHANGES MEAN FOR THE PUBLIC?

The impact of repealing section 230 would have on social media platforms has been discussed in previous chapters, but how would it affect the public?

At worst, sites that allow user-generated content could eventually cease to exist. That means Twitter, Facebook, Instagram, YouTube, TikTok, etc. would all be gone. Sites like Amazon might remain but would probably have to stop allowing reviews. Online shopping? Sure -- at your own risk. The same goes for reviews of restaurants and all other businesses. Want to know what people think of the new shop in town? Well, you'll have to ask them -- in person.

At best, all those sites would still exist but be heavily moderated. The censorship that currently exists in other countries would apply here, but it would be done by companies to prevent lawsuits – rather than the government itself.

Either way, we can kiss freedom of speech on the internet goodbye. The ability to comment on other user's posts would most likely be gone, in addition to heavy censorship on anything anyone posts in general. In many ways, we would end up setting the country back a couple of decades.

Some may argue that a lot of current issues may be alleviated without social media. Watching documentaries like, "The Social Dilemma" makes you wonder how much of an impact the algorithms have had on our extremely divided political climate. There are a lot of things that may improve without the daily effect social media has on people. Mental health, privacy, happiness, spending, etc.

However, if we consider how much our society has evolved around the technology we enjoy today, we must think about the number of jobs that would be lost if those changes occurred. There are social media specialists, strategists, influencers, and managers, and that's just the beginning of the list. How would we replace the income of millions of people? In what ways would this impact an already unstable economy? Many haven't recovered financially from the pandemic as supply chain issues create inflation and prices steadily increase. We also can't forget that social media was one way to stay connected during isolation. There are many variables to weigh when making such a significant decision. Eliminating or changing Section 230 is not as simple as it may appear.

Other countries that are heavily censored are already very shut off from the rest of the world. If we clamp down on freedom of speech in the U.S., we will further the division across the globe. Right now, we can communicate with people in Spain, Greece, and Brazil all at the same time via platforms like Twitter. Without social media connecting us to other parts of the world, we lose that cultural immersion. Most of us can't travel the world to learn about the people living there, but we can through our screens. If we no longer have that ability, think of how to cut off we will be from the rest of the planet. Sure, we can still read books and watch documentaries, but we won't be able to learn first-hand from real people what life is like for them in other parts of the world.

We've become so accustomed to having everything we need available at our fingertips that it's hard to fathom the idea of life without that capability. Have a question? Google it. Need something? Order it. Wonder how someone is doing? Look at their social profiles to catch up on their life. We've taken for granted how social media has allowed us to stay in contact with people we may have never seen again. We have friends from high school, college, and previous jobs all conveniently located on Facebook, where we can see what they are up to and watch their kids grow – even if we don't have time to get together.

Imagine what life would be like without the ability to do that. How many people would you have lost touch with over the years? Perhaps it would make getting together face-to-face more of a priority, but we all only have so much time. What relationships would be worth investing yours into? Probably only a handful.

Networking and marketing for businesses would also be irrevocably changed. Would roles like digital marketing strategist also cease to exist? Would professional sites like LinkedIn make it? What about job boards like Indeed? There are more questions than answers when it comes to Section 230, which is why lawmakers are struggling to make headway. We can only guess at the long-term effects of any legislation that alters the way the Internet functions.

We've seen what's happened in other countries where freedom of speech has been limited. Pakistan doesn't even have dating apps anymore. The latest research in the U.S. indicates that 39% of people met their current partner online. Do we want to limit an already shallow dating pool? It's important to think about every piece of the puzzle when realizing how impactful changes to one law could be, but it's a big one. The fallout from the previous changes already showed legislators that the effects can't always be predicted and that intentions don't always produce the desired results.

The push to dismantle section 230 has slowed as lawmakers deal with other issues that pop up – like the war in Ukraine and the leaked Supreme Court opinion, but the desire for change is still on the table and it will be addressed eventually.

https://bestlifeonline.com/online-dating-divorce-study-news/#:~:text=Online%20dating%20is%20similarly%20popular%20in%20the%20U.S.,compared%20with%20just%2022%25%20of%20people%20in%202009.

CHAPTER 9
WHAT CAN PEOPLE DO?

If people do not want section 230 to be repealed or changed, they need to get involved.

The best way to try to prevent legislation from being passed is to get out in front of it. When you're aware of the issue at hand, you can try to shape the conversation before anything is brought to congress. Although it might be too late for that, if enough opposition is brought up, lawmakers may not move forward with potentially harmful legislation.

Being aware of the legal process is important. Knowledge regarding the path a bill takes to become a law is imperative. Map things out before acting. Research what groups would be affected to connect with others who care about the issue. Encourage people who feel the same way to speak out, write letters, and make calls to their representatives. Look up your state legislators to find out how to contact them. Ensure your team is organized so that everyone is on the same page as far as the message you wish to relay. Unification is important.

It doesn't take an army or a ton of money to make a difference. A small group of passionate people who are willing to put in the work can move mountains.

We've seen how people rally for a cause with all the protesting for the Supreme Court's decision to overturn Roe vs. Wade. Women are out in droves with their t-shirts and signs, battling for women's rights.

Section 230 may not inspire the same level of passion, but it affects everyone. Most people are simply unaware of it and what it means.

Knowing how people feel about it when voting is imperative, and where politicians stand on this issue is going to have a huge impact on society. Be informed and mindful before the next election and have conversations with people who don't know how important this law is and how they would be affected if it were to change.

Regular people often feel powerless when it comes to politics, but one person can make a bigger impact than we can imagine. Think of Greta Thunberg and how a sixteen-year-old, autistic girl made world leaders stop and listen to what she had to say. The average person can accomplish great strides if they are determined enough.

https://americasfuture.org/want-to-make-a-difference-get-involved-in-local-politics/

CONCLUSION

We live in a digital world, where 85% of the population is online every day. In the U.S., our first amendment right to freedom of speech along with a 26-word law passed in 1996 has allowed this system to flourish. Section 230 was created long before platforms like Twitter, Instagram, Facebook, and YouTube even existed, but it keeps them from being held legally responsible for the content that users post on their sites. If they were held liable there would be a lot more content moderation and free speech on the internet would be much more restricted than it is today.

Legislators on both sides of the political divide are pushing for changes for opposing reasons. The right wants less censorship, and the left wants more. Liberals want to crack down on hate speech and fake news, whereas conservative voices don't seem to understand that repealing section 230 would create more censorship, not less.

We've learned from specific carve-outs like FOSTA/ SESTA that it can be hard to see the forest through the trees -- so to speak. Even with the best of intentions, legislation sometimes backfires, and the repercussions can be unexpected. There are a lot of different proposals for ways Section 230 can be changed without repealing it completely. Although there are both pros and cons to making changes to the law, if lawmakers don't consider all the possibilities, the consequences could impact the entire world as we know it.

Any changes made to Section 230 would seriously impact platforms and lead to significantly more content moderation, which would cost social media companies a lot of time and money. Some may not make it. If it becomes too difficult to manage, they may no longer allow comments or reviews on those sites at all. If that happens, some of those platforms would become redundant and cease to exist and along with that, many jobs will disappear. We've seen the impact such regulations have had on other countries and if the U.S. follows suit that may lead to far-reaching global consequences.

If people want to prevent that from happening, they need to get involved and contact their legislators to let them know how they feel. It may make more of an impact than they realize. They can also make sure to vote for people who plan to keep it intact. Most importantly, they need to inform others that are unaware of Section 230 and what it represents. Knowledge is power.

Printed in the United States
by Baker & Taylor Publisher Services